# ARE YOU THE ONE FOR ME?

All scripture quotations, unless otherwise indicated, are taken from the New King James Version®. Copyright © 1982 by Thomas Nelson, Inc. Used by permission. All rights reserved.

ARE YOU THE ONE FOR ME??

Copyright © authors name

ISBN:978-0-9564767-7-7

Published by Vision Media Comm. Ltd
Email: info@colourdesigns.co.uk
Tel: +44 7903 822 987

Printed in United Kingdom

All rights reserved. No part of this publication may be reproduced, stored in a retrieval system, or transmitted in any form or by any means, mechanical, electronic, photocopying or otherwise without prior written consent of the copyright owner.

# Dedication

This book is dedicated to my husband who has always encouraged me to write and believes in my ministry and giftings. Thank you for continuously being an example in ministry by your daily practise of spiritual disciplines and your love for God and the things of God. I appreciate and love you.

Thanks to my two wonderful sons who put up with my busyness and have endured countless singles meetings – you guys are relationship experts already!

This book is also dedicated to the late Pastor Bimbo Odukoya who was such an inspirational role model and an excellent mentor to me; she was the one who first inspired me to minister to singles. It was a privilege to know and work with her closely. I still think and talk about her all the time (much to the amazement of my husband). To me, she will always be alive.

Thanks to God for putting me in the ministry (1 Timothy 1:12) and the awesome gift and privilege of ministering to young people - exasperating as they can be at times, they energise me. I am blessed to be a blessing to you!

# Acknowledgements

Big thanks to the Vision Media team and especially Pastor Ade Adewumi for pulling out all the stops to make this book happen at such notice in time for my 40th birthday. Thank you so much and God bless you!

# Contents

**INTRODUCTION**
**Chapter 1**  Ancient wisdom for modern singles  6

**PART ONE: THE RIGHT FOUNDATIONS**  17
**Chapter 2**  Get advice  18
*(The importance of a relationship mentor and mature guidance)*
**Chapter 3**  Help from above  30
*(The place of prayer and spiritual guidance in identifying the one)*

**PART TWO: PREPARE FOR LOVE**  43
**Chapter 4**  Become a catch *(bring good things)*  44
**Chapter 5**  Go where the girls (or men) are!  56

**PART THREE: NON NEGOTIABLE'S**  63
**Chapter 6**  Look for Character  64
**Chapter 7**  Give it time  76
**Chapter 8**  Create mystery  87
*(The power of purity)*

**PART FOUR: OTHER IMPORTANT STUFF**  102
**Chapter 9**  The more you have in common the better  103
**Chapter 10**  A common vision  112
*(Are you ready to lead & be led?)*
**Chapter 11**  It's a family affair  118
*(The importance of family ties)*
**Chapter 12**  True Love  126

## CHAPTER 1

# ANCIENT WISDOM FOR MODERN SINGLES

It's a tough time to be a single Christian. Single life is a veritable minefield. We live in a world of sexting and facebook - where it's acceptable for young adults to send lewd messages to those they 'fancy' and where singles discover a relationship they are in is over by the change of relationship status of their partner on facebook. There are no rules and anything goes. Serial dating is rife, true love is hard to find and broken hearts litter the pews. Many singles who desire to live right don't even know how to do this – how to navigate single life and identify a life partner in a godly and biblical way. Is there a godly prescription for single Christians on how to find true love and identify a life partner? I believe so.

## Why Genesis 24 is in the bible

As a new Christian I stumbled upon Genesis 24 one fine day and was intrigued. It's the story detailing the process of finding a mate for Isaac, one of the great patriarchs in the bible. In a nutshell, Abraham sends his highest ranking and most trusted employee to look for a spouse for his son. He is sent to a different country to find a spouse and we journey with him as he selects a spouse, meets her family and eventually takes her back home to Isaac.

As a single person (that was 17 years ago) I was curious to discover the ancient customs for finding a life mate that it contained. It was easy to look at it as purely anecdotal and move on but it struck me that it had a deeper significance and relevance for us today. As I read and reread it; it became clear to me that there were principles for modern Christians to deduce from it on everything from where to meet a potential partner to what to look for in a potential spouse and even when to make one's intentions known. I realised it wasn't a chapter to breeze by en route to the weightier matters of the patriarchal lineage.

2 Timothy 3:6 says 'All *scriptures is given by inspiration of God, and is profitable for* doctrine, for reproof, correction, for instruction in righteousness (godly living)........'. This scripture makes it clear to us that God

puts every scripture in the bible for a reason – to give us guidance and instruction to live a godly life and to correct any erroneous beliefs we have in various areas. Thus we can deduce that Genesis 24 found its way into the bible in order to give us guidance and instructions on how to find and select a life mate or husband or wife. And boy do we need guidance in this area! For the past 16 years I have been involved in ministry to singles and the selection of a spouse is a key concern for many singles.

Further, worryingly, many singles are making poor choices. It's not uncommon to see singles choosing life partners based on looks, status or pure desperation. Many are also conducting relationships in a manner that is not godly and which lays a poor foundation for marriage. The statistics bear it out. Christian marriages have the same divorce rates as non-Christians. Research by Barna Group[1] conducted in 2007 found that the divorce rate among Christians in America is 32 percent, which is very close to the 33 percent figure among non Christians. Although the rate amongst evangelical Christians who are defined as meeting the born again criteria was lower at 26 percent, this still amounts to one in four marriages.

---

[1] The study is based on interviews with a random sample of 5,017 adults, age 18 and older, from January 2007 to January 2008.

As pastor's we are constantly dealing with spouses struggling with issues that have their root in poor choice or preparation.  In this book I will share biblical principles with you to help you prepare by being the right person, as well as insight on meeting and identifying the love of your life. We will discuss how to:
- Meet a potential spouse
- Stand out to potential suitors
- Know what to look for in a potential spouse
- Hear from God about a life partner
- Know if a particular person is the right one for you

**Who's who in Genesis 24**
To get us started I have set out Genesis 24 below in The New King James Version (my favourite version of the bible).  The key characters are Isaac, Rebecca, Laban (Rebecca's father), and Abraham and his servant. Throughout this book I will refer frequently to the servant as the matchmaker, so take special note of him as you read Genesis 24. He is the key character as he is the one that selects a mate for Isaac and is a prototype of you and those who will help you in finding the love of your life.

*Genesis 24*
¹ *Now Abraham was old, well advanced in age; and the LORD had blessed Abraham in all things.* ² *So Abraham*

*said to the oldest servant of his house, who ruled over all that he had, "Please, put your hand under my thigh, ³ and I will make you swear by the LORD, the God of heaven and the God of the earth, that you will not take a wife for my son from the daughters of the Canaanites, among whom I dwell; ⁴ but you shall go to my country and to my family, and take a wife for my son Isaac." ⁵ And the servant said to him, "Perhaps the woman will not be willing to follow me to this land. Must I take your son back to the land from which you came?" ⁶ But Abraham said to him, "Beware that you do not take my son back there. ⁷ The LORD God of heaven, who took me from my father's house and from the land of my family, and who spoke to me and swore to me, saying, 'To your descendants[a] I give this land,' He will send His angel before you, and you shall take a wife for my son from there. ⁸ And if the woman is not willing to follow you, then you will be released from this oath; only do not take my son back there." ⁹ So the servant put his hand under the thigh of Abraham his master, and swore to him concerning this matter.*

*¹⁰ Then the servant took ten of his master's camels and departed, for all his master's goods were in his hand. And he arose and went to Mesopotamia, to the city of Nahor. ¹¹ And he made his camels kneel down outside the city by a well of water at evening time, the time when women go out to draw water. ¹² Then he said, "O LORD God of my master Abraham, please give me success this day, and show* *kindness to my master Abraham. <sup>13</sup> Behold, here I stand by the well of water, and the daughters of the men of the city are coming out to draw water. <sup>14</sup> Now let it be that the young woman to whom I say, 'Please let down your pitcher that I may drink,' and she says, 'Drink, and I will also give your camels a drink' — let her be the one You have appointed for Your servant Isaac. And by this I will know that You have shown kindness to my master."*

*<sup>15</sup> And it happened, before he had finished speaking, that behold, Rebekah, who was born to Bethuel, son of Milcah, the wife of Nahor, Abraham's brother, came out with her pitcher on her shoulder. <sup>16</sup> Now the young woman was very beautiful to behold, a virgin; no man had known her. And she went down to the well, filled her pitcher, and came up. <sup>17</sup> And the servant ran to meet her and said, "Please let me drink a little water from your pitcher."*

*<sup>18</sup> So she said, "Drink, my lord." Then she quickly let her pitcher down to her hand, and gave him a drink. <sup>19</sup> And when she had finished giving him a drink, she said, "I will draw water for your camels also, until they have finished drinking." <sup>20</sup> Then she quickly emptied her pitcher into the trough, ran back to the well to draw water, and drew for all his camels. <sup>21</sup> And the man, wondering at her, remained silent so as to know whether the LORD had made his journey prosperous or not.*

*²² So it was, when the camels had finished drinking, that the man took a golden nose ring weighing half a shekel, and two bracelets for her wrists weighing ten shekels of gold, ²³ and said, "Whose daughter are you? Tell me, please, is there room in your father's house for us to lodge?" ²⁴ So she said to him, "I am the daughter of Bethuel, Milcah's son, whom she bore to Nahor." ²⁵ Moreover she said to him, "We have both straw and feed enough, and room to lodge." ²⁶ Then the man bowed down his head and worshiped the LORD. ²⁷ And he said, "Blessed be the LORD God of my master Abraham, who has not forsaken His mercy and His truth toward my master. As for me, being on the way, the LORD led me to the house of my master's brethren." ²⁸ So the young woman ran and told her mother's household these things.*

*²⁹ Now Rebekah had a brother whose name was Laban, and Laban ran out to the man by the well. ³⁰ So it came to pass, when he saw the nose ring, and the bracelets on his sister's wrists, and when he heard the words of his sister Rebekah, saying, "Thus the man spoke to me," that he went to the man. And there he stood by the camels at the well. ³¹ And he said, "Come in, O blessed of the LORD! Why do you stand outside? For I have prepared the house, and a place for the camels."*

*³² Then the man came to the house. And he unloaded the camels, and provided straw and feed for the camels, and water to wash his feet and the feet of the men who were with him.* ³³ *Food was set before him to eat, but he said, "I will not eat until I have told about my errand." And he said, "Speak on."*

³⁴ *So he said, "I am Abraham's servant.* ³⁵ *The LORD has blessed my master greatly, and he has become great; and He has given him flocks and herds, silver and gold, male and female servants, and camels and donkeys.* ³⁶ *And Sarah my master's wife bore a son to my master when she was old; and to him he has given all that he has.* ³⁷ *Now my master made me swear, saying, 'You shall not take a wife for my son from the daughters of the Canaanites, in whose land I dwell;* ³⁸ *but you shall go to my father's house and to my family, and take a wife for my son.'* ³⁹ *And I said to my master, 'Perhaps the woman will not follow me.'* ⁴⁰ *But he said to me, 'The LORD, before whom I walk, will send His angel with you and prosper your way; and you shall take a wife for my son from my family and from my father's house.* ⁴¹ *You will be clear from this oath when you arrive among my family; for if they will not give her to you, then you will be released from my oath.'*

⁴² *"And this day I came to the well and said, 'O LORD God of my master Abraham, if You will now prosper the way in which I go,* ⁴³ *behold, I stand by the well of water; and it shall come to pass that when the virgin comes out to draw water, and I say to her, "Please give me a little water from your*

*pitcher to drink,"* ⁴⁴ *and she says to me, "Drink, and I will draw for your camels also," — let her be the woman whom the LORD has appointed for my master's son.'* ⁴⁵ *"But before I had finished speaking in my heart, there was Rebekah, coming out with her pitcher on her shoulder; and she went down to the well and drew water. And I said to her, 'Please let me drink.'* ⁴⁶ *And she made haste and let her pitcher down from her shoulder, and said, 'Drink, and I will give your camels a drink also.' So I drank, and she gave the camels a drink also.* ⁴⁷ *Then I asked her, and said, 'Whose daughter are you?' And she said, 'The daughter of Bethuel, Nahor's son, whom Milcah bore to him.' So I put the nose ring on her nose and the bracelets on her wrists.* ⁴⁸ *And I bowed my head and worshiped the LORD, and blessed the LORD God of my master Abraham, who had led me in the way of truth to take the daughter of my master's brother for his son.* ⁴⁹ *Now if you will deal kindly and truly with my master, tell me. And if not, tell me, that I may turn to the right hand or to the left."*

⁵⁰ *Then Laban and Bethuel answered and said, "The thing comes from the LORD; we cannot speak to you either bad or good.* ⁵¹ *Here is Rebekah before you; take her and go, and let her be your master's son's wife, as the LORD has spoken."*

⁵² *And it came to pass, when Abraham's servant heard their words, that he worshiped the LORD, bowing himself to the earth.* ⁵³ *Then the servant brought out jewelry of silver,*

*jewelry of gold, and clothing, and gave them to Rebekah. He also gave precious things to her brother and to her mother. ⁵⁴ And he and the men who were with him ate and drank and stayed all night. Then they arose in the morning, and he said, "Send me away to my master."*

*⁵⁵ But her brother and her mother said, "Let the young woman stay with us a few days, at least ten; after that she may go."*

*⁵⁶ And he said to them, "Do not hinder me, since the LORD has prospered my way; send me away so that I may go to my master."*

*⁵⁷ So they said, "We will call the young woman and ask her personally." ⁵⁸ Then they called Rebekah and said to her, "Will you go with this man?" And she said, "I will go."*

*⁵⁹ So they sent away Rebekah their sister and her nurse, and Abraham's servant and his men.*

*⁶⁰ And they blessed Rebekah and said to her:*
*"Our sister, may you become The mother of thousands of ten thousands; And may your descendants possess The gates of those who hate them."*

*⁶¹ Then Rebekah and her maids arose, and they rode on the camels and followed the man. So the servant took Rebekah and departed.*

*⁶² Now Isaac came from the way of Beer Lahai Roi, for he dwelt in the South. ⁶³ And Isaac went out to meditate in the field in the evening; and he lifted his eyes and looked, and there, the camels were coming. ⁶⁴ Then Rebekah lifted her eyes, and when she saw Isaac she dismounted from her camel; ⁶⁵ for she had said to the servant, "Who is this man walking in the field to meet us?" The servant said, "It is my master." So she took a veil and covered herself. ⁶⁶ And the servant told Isaac all the things that he had done. ⁶⁷ Then Isaac brought her into his mother Sarah's tent; and he took Rebekah and she became his wife, and he loved her. So Isaac was comforted after his mother's death.*

# Part 1

# The Right Foundations

## CHAPTER 2

# GET ADVICE
### (The Importance of a Relationship Mentor and Mature Guidance)

*¹ Abraham was now very old, and the LORD had blessed him in every way. ² He said to the senior servant in his household, the one in charge of all that he had, "Put your hand under my thigh. ³ I want you to swear by the LORD, the God of heaven and the God of earth, that you will not get a wife for my son from the daughters of the Canaanites, among whom I am living, ⁴ but will go to my country and my own relatives and get a wife for my son. Genesis 24*

**Find a mentor**
Do you remember the first relationship advice you received? From whom did you receive it? Was it from a glossy magazine, the older boys after a football game or from a television talk show? There are many sources of information about relationships and as a result it is possible to be misled by the varied and conflicting

messages that are communicated from these various sources.

Of all the things you've read about relationships in magazines about how to snag a man, keep a man or catch the eye of the woman you fancy, it's unlikely that you were told that you needed a relationship mentor. Many singles are navigating the minefield of relationships without mature guidance and it is no surprise that many Christian relationships and marriages are failing as a result.

I have found that singles often seek advice from each other. Whilst the advice of other single Christian friends can be very helpful, they often don't have the life and marital experience from which to draw to help you select a life partner. A married relationship mentor can be of great help because he or she should have many practical experiences from which to draw to help you. The advice of a person who is successfully married (and sometimes someone whose marriage has failed and who has learned lessons and is willing to share honestly about their mistakes) can be invaluable.

A relationship mentor will
- help you identify the right criteria to look for when selecting a mate.
- help you draw proper boundaries when dating and

courting.
- help you with advice when you run into difficulties when courting.
- be a source of advice and wisdom on everything from managing sexual temptations to planning your wedding.
- continue to be a blessing when you are married, especially in the early years when you navigate the challenges of being a new husband, wife or parent.

**Focus on the right things**
Most importantly, a relationship mentor can help you direct your gaze at the right things – urging you to ignore some things that are insignificant that you may consider an important negative as a single, as well as helping you to notice some good points that you may have overlooked. I have noticed for example that some younger singles use wrong criteria when selecting a potential spouse. Their focus may range from things like taste in music, fashion sense, looks, sexual chemistry or attraction and the opinion of their friends to the neglect of important things like character, maturity, godliness and suchlike.

**The insight of an older person**
Ruth in the bible may never have made the match with Boaz if it were not for her insightful mentor Naomi who guided her into marriage with Boaz. Ruth was a

foreign girl, a widower and many years younger than Boaz. There were many things that could have been barriers to a marriage between the two. However there were also key points that both Boaz and Ruth were unaware of and which Naomi would use to encourage marriage between the two eventually. Naomi was skilful and took her time to encourage the budding relationship between the two of them. Let's examine how Naomi did this.

*[17] So she gleaned in the field until evening, and beat out what she had gleaned, and it was about an ephah of barley. [18] Then she took it up and went into the city, and her mother-in-law saw what she had gleaned. So she brought out and gave to her what she had kept back after she had been satisfied. [19] And her mother-in-law said to her, "Where have you gleaned today? And where did you work? Blessed be the one who took notice of you."*

*So she told her mother-in-law with whom she had worked, and said, "The man's name with whom I worked today is Boaz." Ruth 2*

**Ruth catches Boaz's eye**
Naomi noticed that Ruth had caught Boaz's attention because of the amount of booty she brought home on the first day from gleaning on his field (a fact it appears Ruth was unaware of). Likewise a relationship mentor

may bring some one to your attention that you have never considered or notice that someone with potential has their eyes on you when you haven't noticed it. My pastor at the time, Pastor Paul Adefarasin, was the one who introduced my husband to me. Although I was reluctant to consider my husband at first simply because he was a pastor, Pastor Paul highlighted his many qualities to me. His wife, Pastor Ifeanyi, also encouraged me by telling me that whilst being a pastor's wife was tough it was a position of honour that I should not shrink back from. I was thus gently encouraged, thankfully, to give some thought to this young man's considerable charms! When I moved to London during our courtship, the baton was passed to Pastor Omawumi Efueye, who pastors House on the Rock, London who we talked with about our relationship from time to time and who took us through relationship counselling. I didn't know it at the time- but they were all my relationship mentors. Anyway, back to Boaz and Ruth.

[22] *And Naomi said to Ruth her daughter-in-law, "It is good, my daughter, that you go out with his young women, and that people do not meet you in any other field."* [23] *So she stayed close by the young women of Boaz, to glean until the end of barley harvest and wheat harvest; and she dwelt with her mother-in-law. Ruth 2*

## Helping you progress with wisdom

When she noticed that Ruth had caught Boaz's eye she urged Ruth to continue to glean in his field instead of moving from one field to another, thus giving her the opportunity to continue to be within Boaz's view and on his mind. She was also mindful of preserving her reputation in the town; that's why she told her not to let people meet her in any other field (lest she get a reputation like the woman in Proverbs 7:11-12 of a crafty woman whose '.. feet would not stay at home. At times *she was* outside, at times in the open square, lurking at every corner'). Naomi wanted to give Ruth, a woman who was already disadvantaged because of her nationality, every chance of being regarded as a woman of honour. Your relationship mentor should guide you to comport yourself in a godly way that will bring favour to you. That's why sometimes pastors and parents encourage single girls not to be seen to be close to a variety of single men.

*¹ Then Naomi her mother-in-law said to her, "My daughter, shall I not seek security for you, that it may be well with you? ² Now Boaz, whose young women you were with, is he not our relative? In fact, he is winnowing barley tonight at the threshing floor. ³ Therefore wash yourself and anoint yourself, put on your best garment and go down to the threshing floor; but do not make yourself known to the man until he has finished eating and drinking. ⁴ Then it shall be, when he lies down, that you shall notice the place where he lies; and you shall go in, uncover his feet, and lie down; and he will tell you what you should do." Ruth 3*

When enough time had elapsed for her character to be established before Boaz and his affection for her to be sure, Naomi told Ruth to give the Boaz the encouragement he needed to make a proposal. Naomi gave her tips on everything from how to present herself to how to behave.

*Then he said, "Blessed are you of the LORD, my daughter! For you have shown more kindness at the end than at the beginning, in that you did not go after young men, whether poor or rich. [11] And now, my daughter, do not fear. I will do for you all that you request, for all the people of my town know that you are a virtuous woman. [12] Now it is true that I am a close relative; however, there is a relative closer than I. [13] Stay this night, and in the morning it shall be that if he will perform the duty of a close relative for you – good; let him do it. But if he does not want to perform the duty for you, then I will perform the duty for you, as the LORD lives! Ruth 3*

Boaz who appears to have thought he was disqualified to marry her because he was old and there was someone with a prior right to her seized the opportunity to marry her when he realized it was possible.

## A modern example

If all this seems a little far fetched, let me share a little modern day example about a young lady I mentored in this area. She had developed a friendship with a young man who seemed keen on her. They had many things in common and enjoyed a rich friendship. She had prayed about the relationship and felt sure that God had confirmed that he was the one for her. However he wouldn't make his intentions clear. He would say things that suggested he liked her romantically and he treated her like a girlfriend but never said anything directly that he could be held to. The young lady was in a quandary and became emotionally fraught as he vacillated between friendship and proposal. She was too emotionally involved and enamored with him to think clearly and decide what to do.

When she came to chat with me about the relationship and told me what had been going on, I told her to sit him down and tell him that she found his behavior confusing because it was clear that they were more than friends but not quite courting. Further, I advised her to tell him that since he was unwilling to put a definition on the relationship, she needed some space and distance from him so that she could gather herself and be free for other potential suitors. He agreed but continued to try to maintain contact with her as before.

I would speak with her frequently and remind her of our agreement that she not respond to his calls, text and emails. When he realized that she was serious about redefining their relationship and that he could lose her, within a few weeks, he told her he would like to court her with a view to marriage.

**Resolving sticking points**
I remember another young lady who came to see me because the man she had been dating was refusing to commit. I asked her to arrange a meeting between all three of us and he agreed to come. The fact that he agreed to come was a good sign and at the meeting I tried to ascertain his intentions. He told me he wanted to marry her but wasn't sure when and that his hesitation centered around the fact that she earned a lot more than him and had a more stable career. At the meeting we were able to examine his fears, explore how they would manage finances as a couple and what things he needed to put in place in order to be ready for marriage. After the meeting she said 'Thank you, Pastor Bimbo. My mother met this man and she never ascertained his intentions towards me or asked him these questions'. They are happily married today. Without a relationship mentor, that relationship would have ended.

Having looked at why it's important to have a

relationship mentor and how they can help you, let's consider what to look for in a relationship mentor.

**How to select a relationship mentor**
Look for someone who
- who is spiritually mature.
- has been happily married for a significant amount of time.
- who is mature and steady in character.
- who is willing to share their marital and relationship experiences with you.
- who is willing to guide you and help you in the selection of a life partner.
- who is available to meet face to face with you from time to time.

This was the criteria that Abraham used in selecting a matchmaker for his son. The matchmaker had been Abraham's most senior employee for many years and was of trustworthy character. He had been overseeing all of Abraham's enterprises and wealth for many years and was well trusted by Abraham. He had also probably been married for many years. He was a man who had a lot of life and marital experience from which to draw from to guide Isaac and most importantly he took the task seriously. He took the time to clarify Abraham's expectations concerning Isaac's life partner and willingly swore an oath to discharge the responsibility according to Abraham's specifications.

Likewise the person you choose as a life mentor must take the task of helping you to select a life partner seriously and must be committed to helping you select a godly and suitable person for you. Your relationship mentor ideally should be someone who knows you reasonably well and whom you can access for practical advice.

Your relationship mentor can be your pastor, pastor's wife, an older married person in your church, a parent, older married sibling or older married friend.

**Great questions to ask your relationship mentor**
- Why did you choose your wife/husband?
- How did you know that he or she was the one for you?
- What have you discovered about marriage that you didn't know when you were single?
- What challenges can I anticipate in marriage?
- Can you share any challenges or difficulties that you have experienced in marriage with me?
- What things do you advise me to do to prepare?
- What things should I look for in a spouse?
- How can I hear from God about a person I like?

### Involve a relationship mentor early

Lastly, there are a couple of other important points. First, it's important to involve the relationship mentor early on, even before the relationship starts if possible. This is important because then he or she has an opportunity to guide you in the selection of a mate and to dissuade from unsuitable people. Sometimes relationship mentors end up simply fire fighting because the couple are unsuitable and shouldn't even be together at all.

### Be real with your relationship mentor

Secondly, in order for your relationship mentor to be a real blessing to you, it is important to be honest with them throughout the relationship. Sometimes singles keep back information or are selective about what information they give their relationship mentor because they don't want to hear certain things. However, the relationship mentor can't help you if they don't know whats going on in the relationship. If you are struggling with sexual temptation, don't have family support or are having conflict over certain things, it's important to share it with your relationship mentor. Your relationship mentor should be able to help you with how to manage or resolve such issues and can even be a go-between or intermediary with family, pastors or your partner. It goes without saying that the relationship mentor can only help you if you take their advice.

A relationship mentor is invaluable – make it a priority to prayerfully find one.

# Chapter 3

# Help from Above
*(The place of Prayer and spiritual guidance in identifying the one)*

¹² *Then he prayed, "LORD, God of my master Abraham, make me successful today, and show kindness to my master Abraham. Genesis 24*

The first thing that the matchmaker did once he started looking for a wife for Isaac was to pray to God for direction. It goes without saying that as a Christian, choosing a marriage partner is not something you want to embark on without prayer. The choice of a spouse is the most important decision you'll ever make (apart from the salvation decision) so it is not one that you can afford to get wrong.

Choosing the right life partner is critical because it will affect everything that you do. It will affect your

- Mental well being
- Your physical health
- Your spiritual life/walk with God
- Your finances
- Your work and career life
- Your friendships
- Your relationship with your family

From the above you can see that the choice of a marriage partner will affect every single area of your life, so it's important to take the time to find someone who will improve your life in all these areas, not make it worse. Unfortunately, as I mentioned in Chapter 1, so many single Christians are making the choice of a spouse based on looks, bank balance, the car the person drives or the kind of clothes they wear. But you'll quickly discover when you get married that fancy cars and clothes are not important when bills need to be paid (in fact they may interfere with bills being paid). It is important to pray so that you are not led away by looks or natural things when selecting a mate.

Whenever single people in our church approach me to tell me about someone they have met, I always ask them if they have prayed about it. Sometimes I detect a mild sneer, indicating that my approach is too spiritual or impractical in affairs of the heart. I am often saddened by this because very few of them know what they are getting into. Marriage is tying your life irrevocably to another person's – you better know what you are doing.

## Get God in on the act

It's important to get God in on the act because God knows the beginning and the end of everything (and everyone).He knows every human beings heart and destiny but we can't discern that as human beings; so the wise thing is to hook up with the person who does. In doing so, you will be able to discern whether the person you are interested in has the same life path as you and if your lives will work well together.

## Praying and hearing from God

So having explained why getting the mind of God on the person you are interested in is important, let's now look at how to go about doing this.

## Praying about it

It's noteworthy that the matchmaker prayed even before he had spotted the girl. Likewise it's important that you pray about your spouse before he or she even turns up. Pray that
- You'll be able to identify the person.
- That the person will spot you – that you won't be hidden.

- Pray that you will be divinely directed to each other.
- Pray that you will not be distracted or led away by people that are not part of God's plan for you.
- Pray that the person will find favour with your family and other important people in your life.

After you've met the person, pray
- For discernment – that you won't be deceived.
- That God will confirm his choice of that person to you.
- For wisdom to conduct yourself in a way that is honourable and holy.
- To continue to have favour with your potential spouse.

### How to discern the will of God

It's good to pray, but that's not enough. You should also look to hear from God – in essence, to have an answer to your prayer. God does speak to people.

*Your ears shall hear a word behind you, saying, " This is the way, walk in it,"* Isaiah 30:21

The key to being able to hear from God accurately is to have a relationship with God. Unfortunately many Christians haven't taken the time to invest in and build a relationship with God so when they need to hear from Him concerning the choice of a life partner they find it hard to do so. In my other book, Relate, I talk about building a relationship with God in more depth, but I will summarise some key points about hearing from God in this chapter so that you understand the various ways in which he can respond to or answer your prayer.

**Scripture**
*Your word is a lamp to my feet and a light to my path.*
**Psalm 119:105**

The most common way that that God speaks to believers is through scripture and God is able to confirm his choice of a life partner through scripture in remarkable ways.

When I met my husband I had another suitor who was a good man that I had known previously and I wasn't sure which one of the two, if any, was God's will for me as a husband. I prayed about it and got on with the regular business of life at that time. A few days later I was preparing for a bible study meeting which I was leading and I stumbled upon a scripture in Isaiah 43:18-19.

[18] " *Do not remember the former things,*
*Nor consider the things of old.*
[19] *Behold, I will do a new thing,*

*Now it shall spring forth;*
*Shall you not know it?*

I knew it was God because I had read that scripture before and glossed over it; but this time it hit me with a thud and had an anointing which it didn't before. That scripture seemed to be indication that I should leave things in the past in the past and embrace the new thing and person He was bringing to me. I saw this as an indication to be open to the new man in my life. I took the scripture as an indication to step into the relationship but I continued to look for other confirmations.

### Dreams

*[14] For God may speak in one way, or in another,*
 *Yet man does not perceive it.*
*[15] In a dream, in a vision of the night,*
 *When deep sleep falls upon men,*
 *While slumbering on their beds,*
*[16] Then He opens the ears of men,*
 *And seals their instruction. Job 33:14-16*

God does speak through dreams. But it is also clear that many dreams can be as a result of the day's activities and normal subconscious activity[2], so the dilemma when receiving through dreams is knowing whether it's from God or you.

---

Ecclesiastes 5:3

I am often wary of dreams of people wafting down the aisle with someone they are already infatuated with because that kind of dream can so easily be a result of one's desires. I would say that unless the dream is particularly spectacular and clearly of God (and agreed to be so by one or two objective people i.e. not your prayer partner or best friend that you have been praying along with for a spouse), you should look for other instances of God's direction in order to be really sure.

**Knowing**
*'But immediately, when Jesus **perceived** in His **spirit** that they reasoned thus within themselves,...'* **Mark 2:8**

Some people say they just 'knew' or perceived when they met their spouse that this was the person for them. Whilst I don't doubt that could be accurate in some instances it's one that's easy to get wrong. Even prophets get it wrong. In Samuel 16:6, the prophet Samuel was sure that Eliab was the person God had chosen when it was in fact David. In a situation where all that the person has is a sense of 'knowing', I would say again, proceed with caution and look for other confirmation that the person you are praying about is indeed God's will for you as a spouse.

**Visions**
*And a vision appeared to Paul in the night. A man of*

*Macedonia stood and pleaded with him, saying, "Come over to Macedonia and help us."* <sup>10</sup> *Now after he had seen the vision, immediately we sought to go to Macedonia, concluding that the Lord had called us to preach the gospel to them.* Acts 16:9-10

This is a dramatic and rare way of hearing from God. Derek Prince, a world renown bible teacher, in his book 'God is a matchmaker'[3] retold, vividly, his vision in which God revealed who his wife would be – a woman that appeared unsuitable by natural evaluation. Despite his maturity in God he took this vision to the men he was accountable to and submitted it to them for confirmation. In the case of such an unusual guide, I suggest the same for singles.

### Peace

<sup>6</sup> *Now when they had gone through Phrygia and the region of Galatia, they were forbidden by the Holy Spirit to preach the word in Asia.* <sup>7</sup> *After they had come to Mysia, they tried to go into Bithynia, but the Spirit[a] did not permit them.* Acts 16

Some other people get confirmation of God's will by a feeling or sense of peace about the intended person and relationship. Peace in this context means having settledness in one's spirit about the person. Another way of defining peace is describing what its not. Having a feeling of unrest or unsettledness in one's spirit about a person or situation signifies a lack of peace. Or when people have a check about, lack of release or a sense of being forbidden to do something, like Paul concerning his trip to Bythnia in the above scripture, then they have no peace.

Many Christians use this means of hearing from God as a guide and whilst it is scriptural it is again not beyond error and should be used as a guide in conjunction with other confirmatory signs.

### Still small voice

*[11] Then He said, "Go out, and stand on the mountain before the LORD." And behold, the LORD passed by, and a great and strong wind tore into the mountains and broke the rocks in pieces before the LORD, but the LORD was not in the wind; and after the wind an earthquake, but the LORD was not in the earthquake; [12] and after the earthquake a fire, but the LORD was not in the fire; and after the fire a still small voice.*

*[13] So it was, when Elijah heard it, that he wrapped his face in his mantle and went out and stood in the entrance of the cave 1Kings19:11-13*

Still others claim that they get confirmation from God about marriage by direction from His voice. God does speak audibly but it takes experience to distinguish Gods voice from other voices.

## Providential circumstances

*[22] So it was, when the camels had finished drinking, that the man took a golden nose ring weighing half a shekel, and two bracelets for her wrists weighing ten shekels of gold, [23] and said, "Whose daughter are you? Tell me, please, is there room in your father's house for us to lodge?" [24] So she said to him, "I am the daughter of Bethuel, Milcah's son, whom she bore to Nahor." [25] Moreover she said to him, "We have both straw and feed enough, and room to lodge." [26] Then the man bowed down his head and worshiped the LORD. [27] And he said, "Blessed be the LORD God of my master Abraham, who has not forsaken His mercy and His truth toward my master. As for me, being on the way, the LORD led me to the house of my master's brethren."* Genesis 24

Some people discern God's will through a number of providential circumstances. Certainly the matchmaker thought that the combination of the positive answer to his prayer request concerning Rebecca which was confirmed by her actions; as well as the discovery that she was Abraham's relative (another important requirement he had) was an indication that she was

God's choice for Isaac.

## Natural indications

*In all your ways acknowledge Him, And He shall direct your paths.* Proverbs 3:6

God can also answer your prayers by revealing things in the natural to you which indicate whether an individual is right or wrong for you. A certain lady told me about an ex fiancée who looked like the total package. He was a successful, outgoing and sociable guy and a real catch. Talk of marriage was afoot then she became a Christian and decided to pray about her relationship and find out if he was the man for her. She prayed and expected God to answer through a visitation or a dream; instead she made a discovery which made it clear he was not suitable for marriage. She discovered a text message he had sent to another lady which revealed that whilst he had been making marriage plans with her he had also been romantically involved with another woman. That discovery showed her that he was unfaithful and deceitful and not the kind of man she would like to be married to.

Having reviewed the various ways that God can reveal His will concerning a life partner, I hope it has furnished you with enough examples for you see to see how God could also guide you in identifying a life partner. Hearing from God is not always mysterious and if you spend time praying, wait on Him and are sensitive to perceive His direction, He will speak to you about the choice of a life partner. God does care about who you marry, because He cares about your life and He has plans to make you fruitful in every way.

*[11] For I know the thoughts that I think toward you, says the LORD, thoughts of peace and not of evil, to give you a future and a hope. [12] Then you will call upon Me and go and pray to Me, and I will listen to you. [13] And you will seek Me and find Me, when you search for Me with all your heart. Jeremiah 29:11-12.*

Some of the methods of hearing from God can bring more assurance than others so it is important to continue to confirm what you heard. In the next chapter we will look at an important confirmatory method of hearing from God which was the key way the matchmaker confirmed God's choice for Isaac.

# Part 2

# Prepare for Love

## Chapter 4

# Become a catch
### (Bring good things)

*[10] Then the servant left, taking with him ten of his master's camels loaded with all kinds of good things from his master. Genesis 24*

*[10] The servant took ten of his master's camels .., loaded with gifts from his master[4] Genesis 24*

At singles events it's not uncommon for those in attendance to be asked to list the qualities they are looking for in a mate. Whilst this is certainly helpful and every Christian should have an idea of the type of person they are looking for and we will talk about this more in a later chapter, it's also important to ask yourself if you possess the qualities an eligible bachelor or spinster is looking for.

---

[4] **The message translation**
[5] **The Message Translation**

It is noteworthy that the matchmaker went looking for a wife 'loaded with all kinds of good things' or 'loaded with gifts'[5] . He took resources of various kinds to show that the person he was seeking a wife for was a person of means and resource, who would be able to look after the girl chosen. Likewise you should have lots of things that recommend you to a potential spouse. So what do you bring to the table? What resources or attributes do you have that indicate that you can be a blessing or a gift to your spouse, and what kind of 'good things' should you be looking for in the one for you?

**Character**
Good Character is a key 'good thing' that you need to bring to the table and look for in the one for you. We will look at this in more detail in chapter six.

**Material Resources**
While it isn't essential that a person is 'loaded' or very rich before getting married, it is important that anyone who is looking to get married is able to provide for himself or herself and is able to manage resources well. Let's look at each point in a little more detail.

**Able to provide**
The truth is that money makes the world go round. Even the bible says that money answers all things[6]. The

ability to earn money is key in maintaining a family and every woman should look for a man who can provide for her family and every man should look for a woman who has the ability to contribute to the household income if she chooses to or when necessary. When assessing a potential spouse's ability to provide consider things such as

- What is his or her past work history?
- Has he or she consistently held down a job?
- Does he or she have a good attitude at work?
- Is he or she diligent and hardworking?
- Is he or she industrious?
- Is he or she committed to developing and improving himself or herself continuously?

These questions are important because they show how employable a person is and their ability to earn or generate income which is a key part of looking after a family.

Several times, couples have come to tell me they plan to get married and neither of them is employed. I always encourage them to wait. It's one thing to be unemployed and single, it's another to be married and unemployed. The latter brings added stress because of the reality of dependants and role expectations for men especially. I know couples who have gone ahead

---

[6] Ecclesiastes 10:19

nonetheless and ended up moving from place to place, bunking with parents and friends and borrowing money here and there – it was not an auspicious or honorable start to married life for them.

This is not to say that one needs to be very rich or have tens of thousands in savings before he or she can get married, but it is certainly wise that at least one of the couple has an income, that they have a small place to rent that is theirs and a little amount saved where possible.

**A person of means**
When assessing a potential partner it also important to consider their attitude to, and how they manage money.
Ask –
- Is the person prudent?
- Does he or she save regularly (even if it is a small amount)?
- Does he or she have any investments or sources of income apart from their salary?

If the answer is yes to at least two of these questions, it is an indication that the person knows the value of money and is able to manage it judiciously. This is very important as financial issues are one of the main causes of marital breakdown[7]. If you are considering someone who often has no money (unless he or she is between jobs), is always borrowing money (from you or others), buys things they can't afford or is constantly avoiding bill collectors- then reconsider! That is unless you want to carry another persons financial liabilities for the rest of your life!

**Appearance**
Whilst looks alone are not a good reason to start a relationship, it's not a minus to be physically attractive. The matchmaker noted that Rebecca was beautiful to look at – Genesis 24:16.

One of the good things you can bring to a relationship is to be physically attractive and well presented.

Research makes it clear that one of the key things that men look for in a potential spouse is good looks[8]. And no women ever turned down a man for being well dressed and groomed!

When it was time to for Boaz to propose to Ruth, Naomi advised her to '..*wash yourself and anoint*

---

[7] Money issues play a significant role in 90 percent of divorces, statistics show say's Ginger Otis in an article titled 'Who's Really the Spender: You or Him?' in Housekeeping Magazine (American edition) April 2011.

[8] What Every Man Wants In A Woman / What Every woman wants in a man John and Diana Hagee

*yourself, put on your best garment…'- Ruth 3:3.* Even for those who are not spectacular looking, you can be more attractive by making sure your personal grooming is good and that you choose clothes that complement your shape and size (and for women, make up that complements your complexion). If necessary, get professional help – there are professional shoppers/dressers in every department store and make up experts who can get you looking tip top.

**Well Developed**
Another good gift that you can bring to a relationship is a well developed 'you'. In order to be a good gift – to yourself and to others- you must invest in yourself and develop yourself in every way that you can.

Develop yourself
- Spiritually – by growing in godliness through bible study, prayer and spiritual growth
- Educationally – by studying and achieving academically
- Recreationally – by investing in sport and other recreational activities that you enjoy
- Physically – by looking after your health and well being
- Socially – see next section

Being developed in all these areas makes for an attractive and versatile person who will be desirable to many people.

**Pleasant personality and behavior**
A pleasant personality and behavior are also highly valuable 'gifts' that are often overlooked. A pleasant behavior is a peaceable and positive disposition. Good behavior includes good manners, hospitable behavior, politeness and considerate behavior. Both are highly attractive. They will make you stand out especially with family members of your potential spouse. Good manners and considerate behavior especially are a sign of a good upbringing and speak very well of the individual who has them in abundance.

It was Ruth and Moses' character expressed through their good behavior that recommended them at first to their spouses or the family members of their spouse.

*[11] And Boaz answered and said to her, "It has been fully reported to me, all that you have done for your mother-in-law since the death of your husband, and how you have left your father and your mother and the land of your birth, and have come to a people whom you did not know before. [12] The LORD repay your work, and a full reward be given you by the LORD God of Israel, under whose wings you have come for refuge." Ruth 2*

*' When they came to Reuel their father, he said, "How is it that you have come so soon today?"*

*[19] And they said, "An Egyptian delivered us from the hand of the shepherds, and he also drew enough water for us and watered the flock."*

*[20] So he said to his daughters, "And where is he? Why is it that you have left the man? Call him, that he may eat bread." [21] Then Moses was content to live with the man, and he gave Zipporah his daughter to Moses'. Exodus 2*

## Maturity

To be mature is to be grown, responsible and able to bear the responsibilities of life. A mature person is not hasty or flighty. When a decision needs to be made, such a person takes the opinions and needs of those who will be affected into account and is prudent and selective in his or her action. Such a person does what is appropriate at the right time and honors their obligations and their responsibilities. Maturity is not determined by a persons age but by their behavior.

Maturity is a gift to a potential spouse because it shows that you will contribute and add to his or her life instead of withdrawing from it. It also means that you are able to participate fully in the relationship and to play your part in its growth and stability.

Maturity is learnt by experience and observation. Work on becoming more mature and look for maturity in a potential spouse.

**Emotional wholeness**
One of the greatest gifts you should look for in, and bring to, a future spouse is emotional wholeness. When a person is emotionally whole, they are healthy and not broken in any part of their emotional psyche. An emotionally healthy person has a positive self image, a good level of self esteem and is not needy of approval and acceptance by other people to a great degree. Such a person is able to give love and receive love freely in a healthy way and without strings attached.

Unfortunately, many people are not emotionally whole. The reasons for this are varied. Emotional brokenness can be as a result of, amongst other things
- Divorce of parents or an unhappy family background
- Past relationship history
- Sibling rivalry and favoritism or preference by parents
- Past poor performance e.g. academically or in sports

- Poor treatment from peers e.g. due to being overweight, unfashionable or unsociable
- Sexual abuse
- Physical abuse
- Emotional abuse

Someone who is emotionally broken suffers from low self esteem and feelings of not being worthy, 'together' or up to scratch because of the things they have experienced. As a result they can end up being unnecessarily suspicious, jealous, insecure, possessive, anxious, or even cold in relationships. Their insecurities and low self esteem can make such a person interpret situations in a way that is unhealthy and inaccurate. For example because of low self esteem he or she can feel jealous if their partner interacts with someone of the opposite sex or interpret statements that were made value free in a way that castigates them.

A person with low self esteem comes to a relationship with a great need for reassurance, encouragement and security. Oftentimes the person they are in relationship with will be required to 'fill them up' by offering assurance that they are valued or by paying them a lot of attention and suchlike. Whilst it is expected that one will express love and acceptance to one's partner in a relationship, the constant need to fill up the love tank of a partner who is emotionally broken can be a constant drain and put a great strain on any relationship.

If you are, or the person you are interested in is, not whole, it is important to give some attention to it prior to marriage and to get whole prior to marriage. The subject of emotional healing is beyond the remit of this book but look out for my other book 'Relate' and my husbands book 'So, who do you really think you are?' which will help you in this area.

**Love, joy and happiness**
A good potential spouse should bring love, joy and happiness into your life- these are some of the good things he or she should bring into your life. Sometimes single Christians are miserable in a relationship because the person they are in relationship with is sponging off them financially, putting them down, abusing them emotionally or physically and yet they stay because they believe God has spoken to them. God gives good gifts and a husband and a wife (even in potential form i.e. before marriage) is supposed to be a blessing not a curse[9].

When all is said and done, a potential spouse should add to you i.e. improve your life and not 'detract' from

---

[9] Proverbs 18:22, Matthew 7:11, Luke 11:13

you i.e. make your life worse in a significant way. While no one is perfect and every potential spouse will have areas they need to work on and improve; on the whole being with your potential spouse should mean that your life is significantly better on the whole.

Ask yourself, since this person came into my life
- Am I better off as a person? Do I feel emotionally, physically and spiritually better than before I met this person?
- Is my relationship with God stronger as a result of this relationship?
- Am I happier?

# Chapter 5

# Go where the girls (or men) are!

*¹¹And he made his camels kneel down outside the city by a well of water at evening time, the time when women go out to draw water. Genesis 24*

I am amazed how many singles who say they want to get married don't go anywhere; that's like wanting to have a baby and never being sexually intimate with one's spouse! If you want to meet someone, go where you are likely to meet someone. It's no mistake that Isaac's relationship mentor went to a place where girls gather to look for a wife for him. You should too.

**Meet people**
As a single person looking to get married it's important that you go out and that you are regularly in a variety of situations where you can meet people. While you need to be careful that you are not consistently 'on the hunt' (which can smack of desperation), you should actively seek out avenues to interact socially with groups of people who could be potential spouses or link you with a potential spouse.

## CHAPTER 5: GO WHERE THE GIRLS (OR MEN) ARE!

While I know that God leads people, we can also ask Him to order our steps into the right social situations. One of my favourite scriptures in the bible is Ruth 2:3 which say's that 'Ruth happened upon Boaz's field...' (and the rest, as they say, is history). She could have stayed indoors with her mother in law mourning over the barrenness of their lives but she chose instead to go looking for work and met lots of men in the process.

You can find love, or love can find you, in many places so don't say no to a social invitation without good reason. Examples of events in which you could meet a potential spouse are listed below.

- Weddings
- Birthday parties
- Church & church events (I know single people who have met their spouse's at church weekend away programs, small groups meetings and whilst serving in the same department in church).
- Work
- School re-unions
- Conferences
- Sporting events
- Music and worship events
- Special interest groups such as a cookery class or a book club
- The gym
- Visiting friends at home

- Visiting friends at work

These are all great opportunities to meet or be exposed to people who could be potential spouses.

**Build a good reputation**
(When asked – what will he or she say about you?)

You should also be aware that other people's opinions of you can be a deal breaker when you meet people at these events. Often someone who likes the look of you and knows someone you know will ask them about you. Let's say you go to a concert or a sporting event with a friend and bump into someone of the opposite sex that he or she knows. If the person you meet is interested in getting to know you more, he or she will often ask the friend who introduced you what you are like. This is one of the many reasons why being of good character and having a nice disposition is so important. It was this kind of report that recommended Ruth to Boaz. Her behaviour and conduct had been so exemplary that when Boaz asked about her he was given a glowing report about her.

This should give us a good incentive to work on our character and be on good terms with all people our paths cross- whether personal friends, work colleagues or those we worship with our church. Each one of those people could be a bridge or connector to your spouse. They have friends and relatives of the opposite sex who they could introduce you to. Relationships with older people can also yield great fruits. I know a particular young lady who ended up marrying the younger brother of an older lady she had become close to in church. The lady was so impressed with her that she was determined to find her a husband and who better than her own brother?

### Internet dating

We can't talk about meeting someone in 2011 and not talk about internet introductions and dating. Everything is done electronically these days and many people are open to the idea of finding love online. The online dating service eHarmony claims that on average, 542 people get married every day in the United States because of them (that accounts for nearly 5% of new U.S. marriages)[10].

### The possibilities are endless

Internet dating does open up the possibility of meeting a wide range of people that you simply would not have the opportunity to meet otherwise. It makes it possible, for example, for someone who has never left Africa to make a love match with someone who lives

---

[10] 2009 U.S. survey conducted for eHarmony by Harris Interactive®

in Sweden or America- the possibilities are endless in this regard. Also because it's increasingly acceptable socially as a way of meeting people more and more people are going online so it's no longer perceived as the domain of loners or desperado's as it was once was. Further some online agencies are strictly for Christians and some like eHarmony have sophisticated ways of matching people based on compatibility and shared interests instead of just looks and profile which is the more standard way with online dating agencies.

**Be cautious**
However, online introduction and dating is fraught with danger and should be approached, if at all, with great caution and awareness of those dangers with a view to minimizing them. Some of the dangers are:
- There is no way of being sure that the person you are meeting is who or what they say are. It is not uncommon for people to be 'economical' about their age or weight or to exaggerate what they earn or the work they do. Indeed grown men (pedophiles) have posed as 14 year old girls online in order to build a relationship with a young girl they plan to abuse.
- Because, in most cases, you have no ties or common links with a person you meet online, there is no easy way of verifying information that they give to you.

- It is also harder to assess the motives of someone you meet online.
- The picture you build about a person from interaction with them online may be a quite different picture of who they are in reality (i.e. even in the absence of any deception by the person).
- You or the person you meet online may like the images of each other in the pictures online but may not find the real person as attractive.
- It's often hard to get a 360 degree idea of a person online as you don't know their family and friends which are an important clue to the sort of person they are.

Because of these concerns it is wise, as said earlier, to approach online dating with extreme caution. However if you choose to go down this route make sure that you keep your address and other personal details private and that when you meet up with the person it is always in a public place until you are very sure about the person. Of course you must also double up your prayer efforts if you are taking this route, asking God to direct you and unveil anything that is being hidden from you. Personally, if I were a single person I would not use this method of meeting people but I had to address it in this book as I am often asked about internet dating at singles events.

**God's got your back**

In closing, it's important to know that God will direct you in your desire to meet someone. It is important not to get anxious about it[11]. Instead pray about it and ask God to direct you like he did Ruth,[12] pray that He would cause your paths to cross with the person that He has for you.

---

[11] **Phillipians 4:6**
[12] **Ruth 2:3**

# Part 3

# Non negotiable's

## CHAPTER 6

# LOOK FOR CHARACTER

*¹⁴ May it be that when I say to a young woman, 'Please let down your jar that I may have a drink,' and she says, 'Drink, and I'll water your camels too' — let her be the one you have chosen for your servant Isaac. By this I will know that you have shown kindness to my master."*

It is important that the matchmaker asked God to indicate the spouse for Isaac by her character. He wasn't just looking at beauty and shape (although she had both), his qualifying requirement was character. What is yours?

**A servant heart**
As the matchmaker sat by the well watching the young

ladies approach, his prayer paraphrased, was 'God give me a woman for Isaac with a servant heart, who's hardworking and hospitable. Give me a woman with an excellent spirit who won't do the barest minimum but who will go beyond the call of service'. His way of determining God's choice was to put the young lady to the test. He thought, 'I'll ask her for water just for myself and see if she is thoughtful, caring, hospitable and hardworking enough to offer water to my camels also'.

To offer to water the camels too would have required thoughtfulness and consideration. The matchmaker was obviously a stranger and had travelled a long way. If he was thirsty, the camels he had ridden in on would be even thirstier. It would have taken thoughtfulness to think about the animals. But it didn't end there; to water the camels meant a lot of hard work. Watering **10** thirsty **camels** would have meant several trips to and from the well because camels consume great amounts of water.

**Is she cute?**
You won't go far wrong either, if you use the same criteria that the matchmaker did. Instead of checking out biceps and triceps and the labels he wears and how handsome he looks when he smiles or how cute she is when she smiles and how delicate and feminine she is

– consider character! I remember one young man who sat in my office as we discussed the choice of a life partner who said 'People go on all the time about character, what I want to know is, is she cute?' Needless to say, he got cute and a whole lot of drama when he got married! Cute just isn't enough. Look for character.

**What it means to be a person of character**
Character means having good moral and ethical attributes. It means a person who does the right things because it's the right thing to do.

The fruit of the spirit described in Galatians 5:22 is a great starting point for constructing the picture of a person of character. A person with good character is
- Loving - a person who is able to demonstrate love consistently.
- Joyful – a person with a positive disposition most of the time, even in trying and difficult circumstances.
- Peaceful – a person who is not contentious and who has a settled and calm disposition and outlook most of the time (even if they are outgoing by nature).
- Longsuffering – a person who is patient and able to bear discomfort.
- Kind – a person who is tender, considerate , thoughtful and helpful nature

- Good – someone who does the right things, positive things and is law abiding.
- Faithful – someone who is loyal, consistent and truthful and able to stay committed to something or someone for the long haul.
- Gentle – someone who is soft (even if they are strong); who is not harsh or brash.
- Self controlled- someone who is principled and able to manage his or her appetites and responses.

**Other elements of a good character are being**
- Hardworking
- Industrious
- Prudent
- Generous
- Brave
- Thoughtful
- Considerate
- Unselfish
- Truthful/Honest
- Consistent
- Diligent
- God fearing

The last point is especially important because it is the root of many of the other attributes that contribute to good character. Proverbs 31: says 'Beauty is fleeting and charm is deceitful, but a woman who fears the

Lord is to be praised'. It was the fear of God that made the Proverbs 31 woman an outstanding wife. It was her fear of God that caused her to
- Gain the trust of her family
- Earn the praise of the children
- Be kind to her servants
- Give to the poor
- Speak gracefully to others
- Be hardworking and industrious

**Fruit, not suit**
Galatians 5; 22 makes it clear that it is the Holy Spirit that produces these attributes in abundance in a person. The more of these attributes a person has the godlier they are. At this point I want to sound a word of caution. Many Christians have chosen people who were outwardly godly- perhaps they had a title such as deacon or pastor, or quoted copious amounts of scripture or prayed for long amounts of time. Whilst all of these are good things, they don't guarantee that a person is godly. The bible says, '...by their fruit you shall know them....' , not by their titles. It is possible by discipline to learn a lot of scripture or to serve in such a way as to procure ordination but the inner man can remain largely unchanged.

Consequently I always encourage single Christians to observe behaviour. Ignore the title and ask questions

such as:
- Is he or she honest in his or her business relations?
- Is he or she well mannered or rude?
- Does this person use clean speech or does he or she use a lot of profanity or swearing?
- Is he or she kind even to people who may be considered socially inferior to him or her or who can do them no favours?
- Does he or she practise scripture, as well as quote them?
- Is he or she forgiving or does he or she /he hold grudges?
- Is he or she quarrelsome and given to bouts of rage?
- Is he or she kind and generous to family and friends or do you notice a pattern of falling out with people or not being on speaking terms with family members and old friends?
- Is he or she person excessive in anyway –e.g. likes to drink a lot, spend a lot of money, or party a lot?
- Is he or she pretentious in anyway e.g. pretending to be lofty or humble?
- Is he or she diligent or lazy in managing his or her affairs?
- Is he or she reliable and dependable or does he or she often not do what he or she says he or she will?

## Character is what you live with

The answers to these questions are important because they determine the kind of person you will end up spending the rest of your life with and the issues you will deal with whilst married. Many thought they married a beauty and woke up with a beast; whilst others thought they married an angel but woke up with a demon. If a woman is quarrelsome and rude as a single lady, she is highly likely to continue to be so as a married woman and this trait will lead to marital strife, problems with in laws and other issues of contention. A man who is lazy whilst single is likely to continue to be so as a married man; if you hook up with that kind of man prepare to spend a lot of your married life motivating him and perhaps dealing with spells of him being unemployed due to a poor work ethic.

On the other hand, a man who is considerate and kind as a single is likely to continue to be so in marriage. In such a case you can look forward to a spouse who will take your opinions into consideration and take good care of you. And if you marry a single lady who is prudent you can look forward to her adding to your household income/ resources and enriching your life in many ways.

Don't be deceived by outward appearance, take the time to discern your intended' character- it will save you a lot of heartache.

## CHAPTER 6: LOOK FOR CHARACTER

**How can I accurately judge someone's character?**
Below are a few things to consider.

**Reputation**
One of the key ways to judge a persons character is by their reputation. What do people have to say about them? Take note of what friends, colleagues and family members say about him or her – what message or picture do you get about this person? Does the person have a reputation as a gossip, for being unreliable, or as a godly and kind person?

**Past and present behaviour**
How does the person behave and treat you and other key people in his life? A person who treats you well but other people badly will also treat you badly once the shine of the relationship has worn off.

Also ask, what is his or her relationship history? If a man has a reputation as a 'player' or for sleeping around, or a girl for being a flirt, don't overlook it – it matters. Take the time to find out if this was b.c. (before Christ) and if they have changed since coming to Christ. If you discover that a person has been sleeping around as a Christian you should be very worried!

Don't ignore warning signs.

### Friends

They say 'birds of a feather flock together' or 'show me your friends and I'll tell you who you are'. Take note of the friends of the person you are interested in, they can give you insight into the sort of person they are. We don't choose our family, but we choose our friends and friendships are based on commonality or shared interests. I remember overhearing a married man saying that his idea of hell was spending the afternoon with his wife's friends because their conversation was so shallow. I wasn't surprised to hear his wife complaining that he never spent time talking with her – he probably thought the same thing of conversing with his wife as he did of conversing with her friends. Your friends reveal who you are.

One of the things that recommended my husband to me when I was single was the calibre of his friends. Once I knew he was interested in me, I started asking around about people who knew him and asking them about him. I noted that all his close friends were people of prayer, ministry leaders and genuinely good people. They spoke well of him.

### Prayer

Ask God to reveal and show you the heart of the person. God can do this in a number of ways – from discovery of things in the natural to the supernatural through dreams and scriptures.

I remember a young lady I had oversight of a few years ago. She had started seeing someone she had been involved with previously. The relationship had ended badly but the man had started coming to church and said that he was now born again so she had started seeing him again. I was unsettled about their relationship and she started avoiding me because she knew I would ask her some difficult questions. When I finally got the chance to speak to her and ask how the relationship was going she mentioned that things were going fine in the natural but that she kept having dreams in which she would see him lying down beside her as himself one minute but the next minute he would turn into a snake. It was clear that God was warning her through the dreams that he wasn't who he was portraying himself to her. However she chose to ignore these dreams. It wasn't until he showed his true colours and was very violent to her that the relationship ended acrimoniously.

**What if he or she is God's will but he or she has a bad character?**
A few times a single person has shared with me that they believe that God has told them that a person is God's will for him or her but s/he has noticed that the person has a bad character. What should such a person

do? The truth is that nobody is perfect and even great husbands and wives have areas of weakness but if you notice bad character to a degree that concerns you, don't ignore it or assume that the person will change once you get married. Having counselled many married women, I have noted that a lot of traits that became big concerns during marriage was detected in the person whilst single but ignored or wished away in that life stage.

**Go back to the drawing board**
In this instance, it's important to go back to the drawing board. Keep praying and ask God to confirm that this person is indeed the right one for you. God doesn't give bad gifts, and although God did tell Prophet Hosea to marry a prostitute - Hosea 1:2, this is the exception and not the rule. Bad character is a key warning sign and cause for caution. In this situation, the advice of your relationship mentor and pastor can be invaluable. Tell them about it and give them enough information for them to get a clear picture of the issues that give you concern. Take any advice that they give you seriously and keep it in mind as you continue to pray.

**Better safe than sorry**
It is also wise in this instance to take a bit of time to observe the person and see if they improve or change

for the better in the areas of your concern. If you see genuine effort to address the areas of concern and improvement with time, then this might be the green light you need to go ahead. But, be realistic about the degree of change and the consequence of bad characters traits when unaddressed. If you continue to be unsettled about it, don't be afraid to walk away–better safe than sorry.

## Chapter 7

# Give it time

[21] *Without saying a word, the man watched her closely to learn whether or not the LORD had made his journey successful. Genesis 24*

When looking for one's spouse it's important not to be in a hurry. One of the reasons that some single Christians are serial daters is because they rush into relationships. Many singles don't take the time to observe or get to know someone they like before getting involved with them. Singles can often be in a hurry because of age or societal pressure; and as difficult as it may be it is important not to let these issues cause one to rush into a relationship. It is not uncommon for a Christian single to spot someone they like, get their number and before you know it, the two are texting, 'pinging on BB' and facebooking each other constantly. It's not uncommon for singles that've just met and are romantically interested in each other to spend hours talking with each other on the phone after just one meeting. Whilst this is understandable, it is unwise.

**Watch from afar**
We should take a lesson from the matchmaker's book. Genesis 24:21 says that 'without a word', he 'watched her closely' to find out if she was the kind of person he was looking for. I always advise singles to observe the person they like without any indication of interest at first. Get to know the person as a friend or colleague first where possible without any commitment. This is important because once someone knows you are romantically interested in them, they may start putting their best foot forward and acting a part instead of just being the person they really are.

## Get to know the person as they really are

By taking the time to get the person without any indication of interest, you get the chance to access the person as they really are. This is what the matchmaker did - he spotted Rebecca as a potential spouse for Isaac, and he approached her not as a suitor but as a netural person needing help.

Singles often tell me that it's hard to observe someone

without getting involved with them. Whilst I acknowledge that it may be hard, its not impossible. There are various ways to do this.

**Observe as an acquaintance**
Sometimes the best way to get to know someone initially is simply to observe them from afar. This is easy to do if you have some legitimate reason to have access on a regular basis to the person without being close to them. Let's say for example that you work in the same office or serve in the same department in church as someone that you like, you have an environment in which to observe them legitimately and without arousing suspicion. I recall a young man in our church telling me how he had first noticed the lady who is now his wife. He served in the same ministry as her sister and observed her kind and gentle manner over the weeks as she waited to pick up her sister on the evenings the choir rehearsed.

**Develop a platonic friendship or acquaintance**
Of course you can always build on observation with friendship at the appropriate time. The key is to be skilled and careful enough to build a friendship without disclosing your intentions! The best way to do this is to keep discussion off romantic issues, not say things that are suggestive and get others involved where possible to throw off any scent of exclusivity or

romance (see more on group dates below). Just spend time with them as friends, get to know them as a person and learn what makes them tick.

**Group Dates**
I often encourage singles to group date instead of going on individual dates as the pressure is off on group outings. Instead of feeling you must be looking into each others eyes as would be the case with just two people on the date; there's the opportunity to get to know each other on a more platonic basis and to observe their personality through their interactions with other people in the group. In a group you can find out, amongst other things:
- whether he or she is shy or outgoing
- how he or she interacts with other people
- his or her ability to hold their own within a group
- whether he or she is a leaders or follower
- his or her readiness to share his or her views


**Ask around**
Another way to observe someone without communicating interest is to find out about them confidentially from people who know them. When I met my husband, one of the first things I did was ask about him from a number of people I knew who also knew him. I spoke to friends we had in common and

my members of my extended family who knew him. From these enquiries I was able to find out useful information about him. I was able to find out, in varying degrees, about his educational background, his academic achievements, his past ministry involvements, his work ethic, his career to date at that time, his personality, who his friends were, his family background and even about his childhood. Of course, this information wasn't conclusive for me but I got a lot that was helpful in determining the kind of person he is.

## The consequences of not observing before getting involved

It's important to take the time to observe someone before making a commitment because it can save a lot of mess and heartbreak. There's a lot of heartbreak among single Christians because they conduct relationships without due care and preparation. Let's look below at some of the consequences of not observing someone before getting involved with them.

### A gamble

The first negative consequence is that when one enters into a relationship with someone without first taking the time to observe them, one is in effect entering into a relationship with a stranger or an unknown quantity.

It's a gamble that could pay off or fail badly. The choice of whom to marry is too important a choice to gamble on. It is much better, because the choice of a marital spouse is such an important decision, to be very sure about it before getting involved with someone.

Some singles enter into relationships willy nilly because they don't think of them as a stepping stone to marriage but as a trial for selection of a marital partner. The thinking is, 'If it doesn't work out then I'll know this isn't the person for me'. Instead the thinking should be ' I am entering into this relationship because I believe it is going to end in marriage'. If that position is taken, more serious thought will be given before relationships are entered into.

**Heartbreak**
The second negative consequence of rushing into relationship with someone without taking the time to observe him or her and being sure that he or she is the right person is heartbreak. Too often Christians are embracing the romance, attraction and rush of meeting someone new and falling into relationships, often involving sexual intimacy. Then after the flush of romance wears off and they discover the true person, warts and all, they have a change of mind and leave the person broken hearted. It is irresponsible and ungodly behavior and God expects much more from

us as Christians. Every single Christian is valuable to God and He cares that they are treated well and honorably. I always say to single men, 'Treat a girl the way you would like a man to treat your little sister'; and I tell single women to 'Treat a guy the way you would like a girl to treat your little brother'.

### Ending up with someone wrong for you

When Christians enter into relationships without proper observation they run the risk of ending up with someone who is, at best, unsuitable for them or, at worst, will make their lives a living hell. This is because sometimes people enter into such relationships and find themselves swiftly swept up the aisle before they can opt out. Consequently, they have a lifetime with which to wrestle with their decision and suffer in compromise or abject misery.

### Low self esteem

When a relationship fails because it was rushed into without proper observation and one of the partner subsequently pulls out, the partner that has been left may suffer from low self esteem as a result. The struggle with feelings of inferiority or worthlessness ensue because someone chose them and then changed his or her mind thereby indicating that there was something wrong with him or her.

**Mistrust**

When a relationship fails because it was rushed into without proper observation and one of the partner subsequently pulls out , it can also store up trouble for when the single eventually does marry. Previous failed relationships can cause mistrust or suspicion of members of the opposite's sex. As a result spouses can find that they are dealing with baggage in the form of assumptions, suspicions and mistrust based on prior failed relationships.

**The benefits of observing before getting involved**

The main benefit of observing before getting involved is that you significantly increase the possibility of selecting the right person and you greatly reduce the risk of selecting the wrong person. Remember – time is your friend. Proverbs 19:2[13] says

'Enthusiasm without knowledge is no good; haste makes mistakes.'

Or in common parlance -only fools rush in!

---

[13] New Living Translation

**A note to the men -making your intentions known**
Once you are sure about the person, don't hesitate in making your intentions known. Arrange to meet with her and let her know how you feel. Give her time to respond to your comments. Try as much as possible to avoid words to the effect 'God told me you are my wife'. Despite the fact that may be true, it can have the effect of putting pressure on the woman by making her feel that she has to say yes because God has spoken. Give her the time to also seek God and be sure about what God is saying to her. It is important that she hear God for herself (and she may have already have done so by the time you make your intentions known), not through your confirmation.

**If she say's no**
The matchmaker gave Rebecca's family the facts that led him to believe that she was the one for Isaac [14]. It was up to them to decide if they would accept the proposal or not. Thankfully for the matchmaker they were also convinced that it was of God and said yes. They could also have said no and if they did he would have had to accept it and returned without a bride or looked for another one. It is important for Christians to understand that even if something is the will of God, if it involves another person the person has free will

---

[14] **Genesis 24:31-51**

and can say no (perhaps because they have not heard from God). God will not overrule anybody's will and it is important to understand this. If someone you believe is the will of God for you is not in agreement, give her time to come round but don't wait indefinitely. If she doesn't change her mind, go back to God and seek Him for someone else.

**Is there only one person for each of us?**
I know of a young woman who had about four men who were interested in her at one time and who were all convinced that she was the will of God to be their wife. One would think at least three of them were wrong. She said no to all of them and they all eventually married other women who they now believe are God's will for them as wives. Is there more than one person for each of us? I don't know; but I do know that God works all things together for the good of those that love him and are called according to His purpose [15]. This means that God knows those who will reject our advances and already has a suitable alternative in place that He will work into His plan for our lives and that are just as much as His plan for our lives as the first person.

---

[15] **Romans 8:28**

**Should a woman proposition a man?**
Lastly, on the issue of notifying one's interest, I am often asked if a woman can approach a man. I don't think it's something to be encouraged because of the nature of men. God made them to be hunters and leaders, and whilst they may be flattered by a woman's proposal, they like the chase. My tip to women is - if you believe a certain man is the one for you, make yourself as attractive as possible to him without being obvious about your interest in him and hope that he picks up the cue.

# CHAPTER 8

# CREATE MYSTERY
*(The power of purity)*

¹⁶ *Now the young woman was very beautiful to behold, a virgin; no man had known her.*

⁶⁴ *Then Rebekah lifted her eyes, and when she saw Isaac she dismounted from her camel;* ⁶⁵ *for she had said to the servant, "Who is this man walking in the field to meet us?" Genesis 24*

The servant said, "It *is* my master." So she took a veil and covered herself.

I recently sat at a wedding and listened, amused, to the chairman's speech. He told us he had been told to take the cue for the length of his speech from a modern young lady's skirt- long enough to cover the important parts, but brief enough to be suggestive! It was funny but a little sad. Sad, because it shows how sexualised women have become.

## Sex and the City

You cannot travel anywhere in any city of the world these days without being confronted with a sexual image every few minutes. We live in a society that sexualises women – our naked bodies adorn paper covers, half naked women writhe on music videos and are used to sell everything from cars to shampoo. For some reason even women in the church are following the trend and leaving little to the imagination in how they present themselves. It appears we have also bought into the lie that we need to show a little bit of skin to get some attention. But in Genesis 24, Rebecca did just the opposite; when she saw Isaac she covered herself. She recognised the power of mystery and purity. Christian singles (male and female) are called to purity and it's a key characteristic you should look for in identifying the love of your life.

## Meaning of purity

*'For this is the will of God, your sanctification: that you should abstain from **sex**ual immorality;...'*
1 Thessalonians 4:3

*'Flee **sex**ual immorality. Every sin that a man does is outside the body, but he who commits **sex**ual immorality sins against his own body'.*
 1 Corinthians 6:18

**Is oral sex, sex?**
Purity means heeding God's injunction to abstain from sexually immorality and to be clean, unspoiled, unpolluted, innocent, set apart and preserved. A single who is sexually pure is one who refrains from sexual activity. I am told that many teenagers maintain that they are virgins despite indulging in oral sex. Sexual activity does not mean only sexual intercourse but includes heavy petting, oral sex and masturbation. Any sexual activity that involves touching sexual organs is part of the act of sexual intercourse.

**Are you sexually awake**
Any single that has a sex life, of whatever colour or shade, is not sexually pure. A Christian single is supposed to be sexually dead. If a Christian single is consistently sexually awake in any way he or she are not pure.

'I charge you, O daughters of Jerusalem, … Do **not** stir up nor **awaken love** Until it pleases'. Song of Solomon 2:7, 3:5, 8:4

This scripture simply states that love (romantic or sexual) shouldn't be awakened till the right time or season. The right time for sexual awakening is in marriage only.

**Sexual thoughts, fantasies and sexy dressing**
Sexual purity isn't restricted to sexual activity but extends to sexually suggestive behaviour and impure thoughts and motives. A person who is sexually pure will have pure thoughts and pure sexual motives. If a single has a sexually active imagination which is often indulged this is impure and sooner or later it will lead to sexual activity. Purity of thought and motives will also show in how one dresses and comports oneself. Many young ladies say they are virgins but their sexually suggestive dressing shows that they are not sexually pure. Rebecca covered herself when she saw Isaac, but these young ladies leave part of their bodies bare in order to draw attention and create a sexual reaction in men. This is wrong and draws members of the opposite sex for wrong reasons.

# The power of purity and mystery

Many singles don't understand the power of purity and mystery- both have tremendous power.

**Purity creates mystery**
Purity creates mystery and mystery keeps people guessing and maintains interest. Mystery holds out the promise of something valuable. When a woman refuses to compromise sexually she cloaks herself with mystery and adds value and interest to herself. Purity

is honorable and distinguishing.

Several times I have seen young men leave women who were sexually involved with them to marry virgins. When a woman preserves her sexual purity she adds honor and respect to herself. By doing so she is saying to the man, 'I am valuable – you can only enjoy me if you'll commit to me'. When a woman gives herself sexually outside of marriage she cheapens herself.

**A young man say's no to premarital sex**
It's not only women who can attract respect by being sexually pure. A young couple who are now married spoke to me about their experience as singles. They had broken up at one point whilst dating because the young man refused to sleep with his girlfriend despite her frequent urging. She couldn't understand why he wouldn't yield; she took it to mean that he didn't love her deeply or wasn't attracted enough to her. He explained to her that it was nothing to do with her but due to his desire to honour God. She broke up with him, but they eventually got back together when she grew in her walk with God.

They got married and she has so much respect for her husband because he showed himself to be a God fearing man who put a priority on sexual purity.

What an example!

## Benefits of being sexually pure

Let's look at the benefits of being sexually pure for single and married life in a little more detail.

**Freedom from fear of pregnancy**

**Freedom from contracting sexually transmitted diseases**

**Freedom from shame and regret**
Singles that are sexually pure do not carry any feelings of shame and regret that come as a result of illicit sexual activity. When Christians who are not married are sexually active, there is always a feeling of shame associated with the activity, especially for women. This is because it is clear that this is displeasing to God. As a result something that God designed to be a gift to be enjoyed and delighted in is polluted. I know women whose sexual lives as married women are marred by the guilt and shame they carry over from pre- marital sex.

Singles that are sexually pure do not have to wrestle with feelings of having been used or taken advantage of by sexual partners. When these relationships end as

they tend to on the whole, the women are often left feeling used and compromised. That is because they have let a man touch them in the most intimate places and then he has turned his back and left. Time and again I've seen girls succumb sexually and lose out. Invariably, the 'brother' ends the relationship and marries a girl who won't sleep with him.

**Freedom to focus on their character**.
When you are not sleeping with someone you get to see the real person, flaws and all, clearly and are not deceived by sexual lust or infatuation. A married lady came to see me a few years ago. The main problem she was struggling with in her marriage was that her husband had been out of work all the time that they had been married and wasn't actively looking for work. She also complained that he was lazy and didn't help around the house. When I asked her why she married me, she looked down and said 'He was great in bed'! Well, after marriage she discovered that his sexual skills didn't compensate for his lack of maturity and selfishness.

**Freedom to focus on the right things**.
When you're dating somebody you're not sexually involved with, you can plan your future together properly as a couple . When sex is not on the cards you have the opportunity to talk about real issues –your

hopes, your aspirations and your future as a couple. When your vision is not clouded by sexual intoxication with each other and your minds are clear, you're able to assess and talk about your future as a couple properly.

**Freedom to invest in your relationship with God.**
When a Christian single is sexually active it affects their walk with God, and impedes their spiritual growth. He or she is often not able to approach God freely because of the sin in their life and a lot of devotional time is spent repenting instead of talking with God. Sometimes the guilt is so bad that such a person totally turns their back on God for a season. But when a relationship is conducted with purity, those involved can approach God boldly and intimately.

**Freedom from soul ties**
When a Christian is sexually pure, there's no issue of soul ties with anybody.

*Or do you not know that he who is **joined** to a **harlot** is one body with her? For "the two," He says, "shall become one flesh."* ***1 Corinthians 6:16***

When someone has sex with another person – their souls are joined or tied together. Because God designed sex to be enjoyed with just one person, even when the two people separate or break up the relationship, they remained joined spiritually because they have had a 'one flesh' experience. As a result many people these days who have had numerous sexual partners are spiritually mixed up because they have been joined or are tied to several people.

A person who is sexually pure is spiritually and sexually intact and unfettered. When such a person finally gets married her or she will be able to give themselves wholly sexually to their spouse; as opposed to someone who has had many sexual encounter and who will have a scattered soul. One man recounted that when he first got married he could not enjoy sex with his wife because sexual images and experiences of other women he had been with would flash before his eyes. He was literally carrying various women around with him in his spirit that were competing with his wife. It took extended prayer and fasting to break free.

### Benefits of purity for marriage

### No comparison
Firstly, if you have been sexually pure there's no one to compare your spouse with so you can't say he or she is good or bad in bed. You don't know anybody else so you don't have anything to judge good or bad by.

**Fewer sexual problems**
Many people struggle sexually in their marriage and many times it's simply because of the sexual experiences that they've had in the past that is interfering in some way of the other with the marriage. For example a married man may still be struggling with masturbation because he's hooked on pornography - a habit he picked up as a single person; or a woman may be struggling with sexual unfulfillment because her husband is a worse lover than her previous boyfriend. It's important to note that one's sexual experiences as a single have a bearing on the quality of your sexual relationship when you get married.

If you remain sexually pure as a single, you are likely to have fewer sexual problems when married.

**Trust**
When you're in a relationship with somebody and you're not sexually intimate with them, it builds trust into the relationship. Let's say you courted someone for two years and never slept with them, it is a great foundation for the marriage because the man can travel for extensive periods and the woman will have peace. This is possible because she knows he has the discipline to hold himself; since he courted her for two years and didn't touch her, she believes he will be able

to discipline himself with other women.

Many times singles think that only single people struggle with lust or being sexually attracted to people they cant be sexually involved with; but even married people get attracted to people they cant be sexually involved with. Managing your sexuality is not only something you struggle with on the side of singleness. Married people also struggle with their purity as well. They struggle with attraction to other people, they struggle with adultery. They struggle with masturbation, they struggle with pornography. Singles who learn to master sexual temptation are better equipped to master it in marriage.

Sexual purity is important for building trust within marriage, ensuring faithfulness and giving a marriage a solid foundation.

## Can you be sexually pure even if you're not a virgin?

Purity is not just for people who are virgins. It is possible to ask God to make you pure even if you were sexually active as an unbeliever. **Purity is something that single Christians can aim for even if they've had a sexual past. Let's look at how you can do this.**

### Watch your heart
Guard your heart above all else, for it determines the course of your life. Proverbs 4:23

The key to sexual purity is alertness – be careful to watch or guard your heart (your thought, mind and emotions).

### Be on guard about your thoughts
Controlling your thoughts is an important part of being pure. What are the things you think about? Note things that trigger certain memories or thoughts that open you up sexually and avoid them. It's also important to be mindful of what things you're exposed to in terms of magazines, movies, TV, talk and association (some people have a filthy spirit) that affect your thought life. If you're reading a lot of magazines with sex articles or watching movies or TV programs with a lot of sexual content, you will struggle with purity. Be careful about the things that you're watching and hearing and also the things you're talking about with your friends.

### Be careful of certain people
Note your feelings and disposition when you are around certain people. If you note that you feel sexually alert anytime you are around someone, take practical steps to distance yourself from them. I saw a

particular girl and guy, two singles, who were attracted to each other and the sexual energy around them was palpable. If you put a match around them it would catch fire, you know spontaneously combust! It was highly dangerous. There was also a lot of sexual innuendo in their communication. If you are serious about purity, you should run from such a person- the only way with them is down.

**Set boundaries in communication**
Draw boundaries early on in relationships, especially in terms of communication. A man or a woman who has improper motives will initiate things with suggestive speech. For example, if a man calls a lady at night and asks her what she is wearing, she should be alert to what he is doing. It's important there and then to communicate that such talk is off limits. Don't be afraid to appear strict.

**Be accountable**
The other thing you need to do is to be accountable. You should have one or two people you can talk to when you feel challenged in this area. You should be able to say to them 'I feel vulnerable at this time, can you please pray with me or can I call you when I feel tempted?' It's important to have someone, of the same sex, who can be there as a support or help for you in this way.

### Staying pure during courtship

One of the best ways to avoid temptation when courting is to be sexually innocent with each other. Do not get into the habit of talking about sexual things or making sexually suggestive comments to each other. If either of you does things or dresses in a way that makes the other tempted, let the person know and insist it be changed. Also do not sleep over at each others place – this is a sure recipe for disaster. If you play at being married, the temptation to do what married people do is likely to be irresistible. A word is enough for the wise!

When courting its may happen that you have seasons when you struggle deeply with sexual temptation. At such times be wise and limit contact. When you do meet, do so in public places where there is less of an opportunity to act on how you feel.

### Get into the word

I remember a listening to a message a man preached. He said he had an issue with masturbation that he had struggled with for years. He said the problem was handled by studying scripture. He got into God and God's word and began to get revelation and understanding; it took him some time to realize that weeks had passed and he hadn't masturbated. His gaze had so moved from his own fleshly needs to God and things of God that the sexual appetite fell off him without him even realizing it.

Many times when people fall sexually it's because they are in a season when they're spiritually tired or dry and their focus on God is not strong. Alternatively, it might be a time when they're away from their usual environment (e.g. a move to a new city or a holiday away from home) and don't have the normal spiritual routines and support or accountability structure that keeps them on the straight and narrow.

**Pray about it**
Lastly, don't feel that you cannot pray about your feelings; if you're having challenges with sexual temptation-pray about it. Tell God 'I want to be faithful to You, I want to be pure. I want to honor You with my body; please help me Lord in this situation. I don't know what you're going to do Lord but please give me strength'. He can handle it and He'll help you because your purity glorifies Him.

# Part 4

# Other important stuff

# CHAPTER 9

# THE MORE YOU HAVE IN COMMON THE BETTER

*Abraham spoke to the senior servant in his household, the one in charge of everything he had, "Put your hand under my thigh and swear by GOD – God of Heaven, God of Earth – that you will not get a wife for my son from among the young women of the Canaanites here, but will go to the land of my birth and get a wife for my son Isaac." Genesis 24*

The modern reader of this verse may wonder why Abraham was so particular about where the spouse for Isaac should come from. In a nutshell it is because he wanted Isaac's wife to come from a line of people that he had a lot in common with and a common destiny with. Let's look at both of this in detail.

Abraham wanted the wife for Isaac to come from his country because he wanted someone from a similar background to his, who would be familiar with the customs, ways and history of the clan. Marriage is so tough and there are so many areas that couples have to navigate and work on that a couple who already have areas of agreement or similarity have a head start.

I remember watching a movie of what was originally an 80's TV series. In the movie remake, an undercover cop who infiltrates a group of drug dealers in order to bring down their cartel falls in love with one of the gang who is female. She falls in love with him too unaware of his true identity. I watched enthralled by the depth of feeling between them and curious as to how the relationship would end- aware that neither could survive for long in each others' world. At the end of the movie, with the cops true identity revealed, the two had to go their separate ways despite the deep love they had for each other. Their worlds were simply too different for both of them to live happily together.

The truth is that love is not enough to sustain marriage, having many things in common is key. Research shows that the more a couple have in common, the higher the likelihood that their marriage will succeed. Neil Clark Warren, is a psychiatrist who has carried out research on thousands of successful marriages as well as 500 divorced couples to find out what makes a marriage succeed or fail. His research showed that similarity or compatibility in key areas is crucial for a successful marriage. I list a few of them below

1. Similar energy levels
2. Similar family background
3. Similar levels of intelligence
4. Similar educational background
5. Similar levels of ambition
6. Similar values and outlook on life
7. Similar spiritual beliefs.

**Similar energy levels**
Have you ever heard the saying, 'My get up and go has got up and gone?' Well, imagine living with someone who continuously has low levels of energy whilst you are always full of beans and raring to go. Before long you'll be feeling weighed down and as if you're being held back. If these feelings aren't managed, irritation with, and resentment towards, your partner can quickly build. That's why it's important to look for someone who has a similar level of energy or the same amount of zest for life that you do.

### Similar family backgrounds
A couple who have similar backgrounds are likely to have had similar levels of exposure and are likely to have similar expectations about role or family structure for example. We will look at this more in a later chapter.

### Similar levels of intelligence and educational achievement
Likewise a couple with similar levels of intelligence or educational achievement is likely to be able to converse about subjects at similar levels of depth or understanding. There is also likely to be less possibility of feelings of inferiority or superiority amongst either partner which can cause strife and disagreement.

### Similar levels of ambition
Many marriages break up because the couples want different things out of life. One person may be very driven and willing to work hard and put a lot of effort into achieving goals, whilst the other person may desire to just take life one day at a time. Such a couple will of course run into difficulty sooner or later.

### Similar vision
In the next chapter we will look at the importance of a common vision.

### Similar interests

About 10 years ago a couple came to see me. The lady was a real fashion plate whilst the man was an academic who spent all his money on books and had no interest in fashion. I had fears for their relationship because they had little in common. When a couple build a relationship on attraction and have little in common, once the attraction wears off, there is little to hold the marriage together.

Friendship is the real glue of marriage and a couple who are romantically linked should also have a strong friendship aside of the romance. Friendship is built on common interests, shared humour and regard and respect for each other. All these things can remain and continue to be shared by the couple long after the shine of romance has worn off.

### Can two very different people have a successful marriage?

This is not to say that people who are very different cannot have a successful marriage. However they will encounter more difficulties and must be willing to be very flexible and work hard to make the marriage a success. I have found that even people from the same country but from two different ethnic tribes can encounter many difficulties based on language and differing cultural expectations and outlooks. To make it work such a couple must have a deep love for each other, excellent communication and conflict resolution skills and unswerving commitment to each other.

## Have a common destiny

The bible makes it clear that Christians are not to marry people from other religions. I know it is not fashionable or inclusive to say so, but that is what the scripture says.

*Do not be **unequally yoked** together with unbelievers. For what fellowship has righteousness with lawlessness? And what communion has light with darkness? 2 Corinthians 6:14*

**Why does God say this?**
The second reason that Abraham wanted a wife for Isaac from his country was because he didn't want Isaac to be led away spiritually by involvement with someone with different spiritual beliefs. The Canaanites amongst whom he lived worshipped a multitude of idols, and lived, and offered sacrifices to their Gods, in detestable ways.

Moreover, because they didn't know Abraham's God and His ways, any woman from there wouldn't be able to live in a way that would ensure that the family entered into the destiny He had in place for Isaac. Isaac had a destiny in and with God and hooking up with someone who didn't worship his God would mean that he wouldn't see the fulfillment of God's promises. That is also true for many believers today when they marry people who are not Christians.

I know many Christians find it hard but the truth is that it's hard to serve God wholeheartedly when you are with someone who doesn't worship the God that you do.

Imagine
- sharing your life with someone who doesn't reverence Jesus.
- not being able to attend church regularly with your spouse.
- not being able to agree in Jesus name with your partner.
- not being able to share a revelation from scripture with your spouse knowing he or she'll understand and be able to contribute.
- the Holy Spirit not having access to your spouse to guide, instruct and warn them.
- not being in agreement about how your children will be saved and reared spiritually.
- the spiritual forces that are opened up into your home by having worship of another god.

Marrying someone of a different faith leaves the door open for disunity in marriage. I know many Christians who married Muslims, for example, who have struggles in their marriage over how their children should be raised, what food and clothing is permissible in the house, how to worship and even what the role of the woman is in the home. It is not uncommon for a Christian married to a Muslim to share her husband with several other women because his faith permits it. The question of the religion of who you marry is very important and should not be glossed over.

**Someone of no faith**

Also worthy of note, is the risk inherent in marrying someone with no faith. There are many wolves in sheep's clothing in the church – who say they are Christians but are not. Do not determine that someone is a Christian just because they come to church, speak 'Christianese' or say they are. You can only judge someone to be a Christian when you see Christ in them. Make sure that you take the time to confirm that the person has a living relationship with Christ before joining yourself to him or her. I have known stark unbelievers to come to church seeking a wife with the full intention of returning to their former lifestyle after marriage.

As a single Christian I met a man who had been an acquaintance for years but who I hadn't seen for a while. After he discovered that I was a Christian he asked if he could come to church with me. We met up and went to church a few times and he would call me afterwards and ask questions about Christianity and appeared to have a deep interest in becoming a Christian. This went on for a while. I later found out that this was all a ruse and all the time he had been coming to church he had continued to be live a very hedonistic lifestyle. He had no intention of becoming a Christian and was only coming to church in order to snag me.

Be careful to seek a man (or woman) after God's (Jesus') heart not just yours.

## CHAPTER 10

# HAVE A COMMON VISION

*And the servant said to him, "Perhaps the woman will not be willing to follow me to this land. Must I take your son back to the land from which you came?"*

*6 But Abraham said to him, "Beware that you do not take my son back there. 7 The LORD God of heaven, who took me from my father's house and from the land of my family, and who spoke to me and swore to me, saying, 'To your descendants[a] I give this land,' He will send His angel before you, and you shall take a wife for my son from there.*

*8 And if the woman is not willing to follow you, then you will be released from this oath; only do not take my son back there." Genesis 24*

By insisting that the woman come to him instead of Isaac going to be with her, Abraham was making it clear that the woman who married him must acknowledge his headship and be willing to fall in line with his vision. Let's look at two important aspects of this – the importance of vision for singles when identifying the one for them and the issue of headship and submission.

## Vision

It is important that the man, who God as designated as the head of the family unit[16], has a clear vision and focus for his life. One key thing that every leader must have is vision; no one can lead without a vision. The problem with many marriages these days is that we have men (leaders) without a vision for themselves, talk less of their family. This couldn't be said of Isaac – he had a clear vision and mandate from God for his life.

## Why is vision important?

A man having a vision for his life is important because he is the leader or the head of the home. Liberation or not, many women still expect their men to be the main bread winners and to be the 'rock' of the family. Women want a man they can look up to, depend on and seek for direction at key times[17]. I have seen many

---

[16] **Ephesians 5:23**
[17] What men want in a woman/ What women want in a man – John and Diana Hagee

marriages falter because the husband doesn't have a vision for his life. When a man doesn't have a vision for his life, the whole family lacks direction and stability.

I know of numerous men who stumble from job to job with passing trends – one day they're business men, then they are information technology specialists, then property investors. Each job change is interspersed with months of studying and investing of family savings in the latest venture or worse still spells of unemployment, brief or prolonged. During these times the wife may have to carry the burden of being the home maker and main breadwinner. The weight of this over time can put great strain on a marriage.

*[7] Even things without life, whether flute or harp, when they make a sound, unless they make a distinction in the sounds, how will it be known what is piped or played? [8] For if the trumpet makes an uncertain sound, who will prepare for battle? I Corinthians 8:7-8*

What this scripture is saying is that it's hard to follow anything that is not strong and clear in the directions it's giving. A trumpet had to be blown to sound a certain way in order to alert to prepare for war. Likewise for a man to be able to rouse and direct his family he must have a clear and consistent voice. His family should know what to expect from him because his vision over the years has been clear, consistent and made well known to them over time (which will be difficult if the vision is always changing). This breeds trust and respect.

One of the greatest things a man can do is discover a clear vision for his life and develop the consistency and strength as a leader to stick with it to see it come to pass.

A woman should look for a man who has a clear vision for his life and whom she respects.

**Headship and submission**
Headship and submission are difficult topics to talk about these days. We live in a post modern age in which women can do anything a man can do (and sometimes better). There are no longer clearly defined roles for either sex. Women lead large corporations and some men are house husbands.

Whilst it's not my intention to drive us, kicking and screaming, back to the 1950's, it is clearly this fluidity of, and lack of clarity about, roles within the family that is responsible for much of the family breakdown that is now commonplace in our society. People come to marriage with different assumptions about what role they will play and disagreement about this or unwillingness to assume a role that the other party expects causes problems. No one who is serious about having a strong marriage should neglect discussion and agreement about this important issue.

The bible is clear that God has called men to be the head or leaders of their family. The Christian man is called to steer the ship of the family, with the assistant of his wife. Many women nowadays take issue with the idea of men as heads of the home. It will help if we can understand God's mind and heart on this matter.

**Unity not division**
Firstly, it's important to understand that leadership is a trust. Any man who brags about leadership does so because he doesn't appreciate what is involved.

[25] Husbands, love your wives, just as Christ also loved the church and gave Himself for her, Ephesians 5:25a
 Leadership is about sacrifice and service. In leading his family, a man is called to make their wellbeing and care his priority. When women understand leadership to mean this- it is easier to submit to.

Secondly, it's hard for a marriage to survive with two different visions because two different visions will pull a family in two different directions. That is why God calls the man to be the head of the family and to be the primary visionary. This however this doesn't mean that the women can't have a vision for her life. I think that women object to the idea of headship and submission because they think it means losing oneself; but that's not Gods plan for women. God also gives women a vision and a plan for their life and the key is to look for a man with a vision she buys into and within which she can subsume her own vision. Abraham invited the woman into the vision for Isaac's life. She was welcome to embrace it and journey (literally) into it with her or she could reject it and stay in her country.

A woman should look for a man whose vision gets her excited and within which she can see herself and find her own fulfillment. When she does this submission will be considerably easier to embrace and she can look forward to a fruitful married life.

A man should look for a woman who embraces his vision and can amplify and contribute to it; and who is willing to follow his leadership.

## CHAPTER 11

# IT'S A FAMILY AFFAIR
*(The importance of Family ties)*

*⁴ but you shall go to my country and to my family, and take a wife for my son Isaac." Genesis 24*

Couple's often think that their marriage is just about the two of them; but there are so many more people involved. African culture sees marriage as the coming together or joining of two families and that is a more accurate picture of the reality of married life. Lets take a look at two important aspects of family ties – family background and family approval.

**Family background**
It's important to give some thought to the family background and values of a person you are

considering marrying. This is because family background often shapes individuals whether they are aware of it or not and influences how the individual relates to their spouse and raises a family. That is why Abraham wanted a spouse from his clan – because he knew she would bring values and traits that he was familiar with and that was important to him. Likewise when you check out someone's family background you should be looking for clues into your future with them. That is you are trying to identify trends or issues or patterns, good or bad, that will be a part of your life, if you marry that person, as a result of that person's family background.

**When considering someone's family background, things to consider include**

**1. What is their family known for?**
For example some families are known for being socialites; so consider if you will be expected to live that kin of lifestyle and if you are happy to.

**2. What is their family reputation?**
I recently watched a TV program about the Kennedy's. When Jacqueline Onassis was dating John Kennedy, her mother told her 'His father is an adulterer and he has raised his boys to be like him – to take what they want, use it and discard it. He

will never be faithful to you'. She ignored the advice and suffered greatly from his serial adultery throughout their marriage.

3. **Are they traditional or anglicised/modern in their outlook?**
   This will tell you a lot about how you are expected to relate with, and address, family members. For example in our family we are quite traditional in the area of how we address people and rarely call anyone older than us (even by a few years) by name; whereas in my husbands family everyone is addressed by their first name irrespective of age. Whilst courting I had to advise him how to address my older siblings and have never been able to bring myself to call his oldest brother or sisters by name.

4. **Are there any peculiar or outstanding family traits or patterns?**
   For example in some families all the children work for the father. In such a case it would be good to examine the nature of the working relationship and if a personal/ work dichotomy exists and if the children have any independence.

5. **What are their mother and father like?**
   Are they domineering or relaxed? Is their marriage good or bad and why?

6. What are their siblings, and their marriages, like?
   If all the siblings are happily married or divorced, it gives you a clue as to what you may experience.

7. **What are the family customs?**

8. **Do the family have any expectations of spouse's?**
   For example, in some families there may be a pattern of female spouses not working. If a woman marrying into the family plans to work this may be a problem within that family.

9. **What is their heritage – spiritual and natural?**
   Sometimes there is a strong history of occult practice in a family. It is important to note this as that invariably means that spiritual warfare will be on the cards at some point in your marriage.

10. **Are there any health issues within the family?**
    There may be a history of mental illness or sickle cell for example in a family that would be important to know and could sway your decision to choose that person.

11. **Are there patterns of failure or success in the family and if so, in what areas?**
    One lady mentioned that she noticed a pattern of men dying around the age of 40 in her family. That

would be an important point for someone marrying into that family to know.

12. **Does the person you are considering identify strongly with family traits and patterns or do they stand apart in some way and is this a positive or negative thing?**

    When all is said and done, some people do buck family trends and patterns. In the example above about the Kennedy's one of the brothers remained faithful to his wife throughout his marriage and regularly chided his brothers for their adulterous behaviour.

**Family approval**

Another important point when looking at the issue of family ties is parental approval. Marriage is tough enough without opposition within your camp. Where possible you should seek the approval of your family of the choice of partner. If not you could be in for years of in-law trouble which you do not want. You must realize that each person's family is very important to them. If a family don't like one of the individuals spouse, the individual's loyalties will be divided and this will be a source of great tension and division between the individual and his or her spouse. Also when you get married your families will spend time together at important times such as birthdays, Christmas and Easter seasons and other key times so good relations is key.

**Go where you are celebrated**
I know a young man who believed so strongly that a certain young lady was God's will for him. They were in love with each other but her family couldn't stand him. Whenever he called, they wouldn't pass on his messages to her and when he visited her, her brothers would leave him waiting at the door for ages. He experienced so much humiliation from the family. He finally gave in and broke up the relationship because of the family resistance despite what he believed God had said to him. A year later he met another woman. The first time he visited her at home all the family came and sat with him and made him feel so welcome. He was overwhelmed by their warmth; he didn't know what he had been missing. He told me after that, 'Tell singles to go where they are celebrated'. He realized that if he had married the first girl it would have been like moving into a war zone. Now he is happily married to the second woman and her family is like his own. Family support is important. That is why the matchmaker made it a priority to find out what the family thought of the match at the earliest opportunity and so should you.

### The counsel of pastors

It is also important not to overlook the counsel and guidance of pastors. Because pastors have guided and counseled many couples over the years they have a lot of insight into relationships. Also, if a pastor knows the person you are interested in and is not supportive of the relationship, you should be cautious as they probably know something that you don't that is not positive about the individual but which they can't divulge for reasons of confidentiality.

A while ago a lady came to see my husband and 1. She had married her husband against the counsel of her pastor and they had eloped together. After a brief honeymoon period, he stopped going to church and became a philanderer. A little while later he moved another woman into their home and dared her to do anything about it.

It's important to take the opinions of those close to you to heart. Their approval and disapproval should be important factors in your selection of 'the one'. If they don't approve of someone you are interested in, it's important to try and find out why and what you can do to correct any erroneous beliefs or misconceptions they have about the person. If the person is truly God's will for you, he or she will eventually win them over.

I know a young lady whose family disapproved of her boyfriend at first when they were courting. However he was persistent and invested heavily in building relationship with her family. When they saw how well he treated her and his humility in continuously reaching out to them despite their attitude towards him they embraced him. However if despite your best efforts, the person you likes family do not accept you, reconsider.

Remember – it's better to go where you are celebrated.'

# CHAPTER 12

# TRUE LOVE

*He married Rebekah and she became his wife and he loved her. Genesis 24:67*

I hope from this book that you've learnt that the selection of a life mate is a serious decision and that you have garnered a few tips that will help you identify Mr. or Miss Right when he or she comes along. I also hope it's shown you how you can be prepare to be someone's Miss or Mr. Right.

It's important to note that love shouldn't be too much hard work, at least at the beginning. If a relationship has to be forced or invested in heavily at the start, it probably isn't 'the one'. A divine relationship has an element of 'magic' to it, in the sense of things falling into place with relative ease – almost as if there's someone behind the scenes causing everything to fall into place ( because there is), even when there are surrounding difficulties.

Last but not least, remember that the core of marriage is love. Make sure that you have a genuine and true love for the person you marry. Today too many Christians compromise- they marry because they are getting old, want to have a baby or are ready to make do with Mr. or Miss Available instead of waiting for Mr. or Miss Right. Sure, love may not hit you in the eye the first day you meet, but love should grow as you get to know each other and be settled in your heart by the time you say 'I do'. One of the most beautiful scriptures in the bible is Genesis 29:19 which says *'So Jacob served seven years for Rachel, and they seemed only a few days to him because of the love he had for her'.* This scripture conveys to us the depth of love that God intends for married couples to have for each other. It is possible to find such love when we take our time and choose well.

The previous chapters were written in order to guide your path to true love. Far from pure emotion, hormonal reaction or flighty feelings; true love is concrete and measurable. This is what it is – unselfish, caring, forgiving, tender, hopeful and true.

*Love never gives up.*
*Love cares more for others than for self.*
*Love doesn't want what it doesn't have.*
*Love doesn't strut,*
*Doesn't have a swelled head,*
*Doesn't force itself on others,*
*Isn't always "me first,"*
*Doesn't fly off the handle,*
*Doesn't keep score of the sins of others,*
*Doesn't revel when others grovel,*
*Takes pleasure in the flowering of truth,*
*Puts up with anything,*
*Trusts God always,*
*Always looks for the best,*
*Never looks back,*
*But keeps going to the end.*
*Love never dies*[18]

I pray that you will find true love, first from above and then here on earth.

---

[18] I Corinthians 13: 3-10- The message translation